TENTERDEN & DISTRICT

THROUGH TIME

Naomi Dickins

AMBERLEY PUBLISHING

Acknowledgements

I would like to thank the Tenterden Museum for allowing me full access to their photographic archive and, in particular, Debbie Greaves for her unfailing generosity, patience and encouragement. Thanks, also, to Tenterden Town Council for the use of their photograph collection and the Bethersden Local History Society for allowing me to reproduce the photographs of Bethersden included here, all of which belong to the Society.

Any mistakes – for which I make my apologies – are entirely my own.

For Paul, and for Grace and William
with my thanks for your loving support in all I do.

First published 2013

Amberley Publishing
The Hill, Stroud, Gloucestershire, GL5 4EP
www.amberley-books.com

Copyright © Naomi Dickins, 2013

The right of Naomi Dickins to be identified as the
Author of this work has been asserted in accordance with
the Copyrights, Designs and Patents Act 1988.

ISBN 978 1 4456 2119 7 (print)
ISBN 978 1 4456 2128 9 (ebook)

British Library Cataloguing in Publication Data.
A catalogue record for this book is available from the
British Library.

Typesetting by Amberley Publishing.
Printed in Great Britain.

Introduction

The story of Tenterden begins in a clearing cut into an ancient forest, its chapters chronicling the lives of industrious cloth weavers and wealthy merchants; royal shipbuilders and daring smugglers; independent theologians; hard-working farmers and enterprising business entrepreneurs. From this rich history has emerged the Tenterden of the twenty-first century – a prosperous and elegant market town in the heart of the Kentish weald.

From the late 600s, it was to this den that the men of Thanet drove their pigs to feed during the winters, and it is from this tradition that the area receives its name, 'Tenet-warre-den': the den of the men of Thanet. The Minster at Thanet had appropriated this land in the unsettled low weald and now began to manage it. As the forest was cleared, so the Romney Marshes were gradually reclaimed, revealing rich grazing lands; these would provide the foundations from which a hugely successful industry in sheep farming and cloth manufacture was to grow from the twelfth century. For over 300 years, the manufacture of English broadcloth – a luxury commodity exported across the Continent – was centred on Tenterden, Cranbrook and their surrounding villages. Truly a cottage industry, the various stages of cloth production were carried out within the home, and it is due to this activity and the prosperity it brought that there are so many splendid examples of Wealden hall houses of the Tudor period in the area. In addition to these grand houses, there are many examples of the workshop-houses of weavers, easily identified by their characteristic steeply-pitched roofs, designed to accommodate the large broadcloth looms.

Other environmental changes were to have a different sort of impact on Tenterden; in the late thirteenth century, the course of the River Rother was altered by a number of violent storms; the port of Romney lost its significance, and smaller ports – such as Smallhythe – flourished in its stead. Tenterden was granted a Charter of Incorporation into the Cinque Ports in 1449 in order to help restore the strategically important but impoverished port at Rye. For nearly 300 years, the town prospered from its maritime connections, but the English shipbuilding industry was being gradually transferred to the west of the country and so Tenterden returned to its farming tradition.

During the seventeenth and eighteenth centuries, the religious upheavals that racked the Stuart monarchies and the Commonwealth reverberated with particular strength in the South East. Across the low weald, the abundance of nonconformist churches, chapels and meeting houses is a remarkable feature, with even the smallest towns and villages boasting a wide variety of places of worship; in Tenterden and the villages around there are particularly strong Baptist and Methodist links.

The Victorian and Edwardian eras brought Tenterden prosperity and modernisation. In common with other rural communities throughout the 1800s, the population of Tenterden suffered a decline as people migrated to larger towns in search of work and cheap accommodation. However, a thriving farming culture sustained the town, its annual stock fair and regular markets and a confident, independent town council initiated improvement projects such as the refurbishment of the town hall and the installation of telegraph wires before the First World War. This was also the period that witnessed the transformation of the hamlet of Boresisle into the village of St Michael's, and it was in 1900 that Tenterden's inhabitants gained access to the Rother Valley Railway. From the turn of the twentieth century, the district's population entered into a period of steady growth, which was reflected in the increasing commercialisation of the town centre.

For the past century and a half, photographers have been capturing and preserving scenes of daily life, unremarkable snapshots in their own time but providing – when examined in comparison with contemporary Tenterden – fascinating evidence of the developments that have shaped the surroundings into the town and district it is today.

Heronden Hall Gatehouse, West Cross

The ancient manor of Heronden can be traced back to a charter of 968, when it was in the possession of Queen Aethelflaed. This imposing arched, stone entrance (recently restored) marks the far west end of the High Street. It was part of the new Heronden Hall, built in the 1800s by Mr Whelan, and stands on or near the site of a Tudor house that had been demolished in the late 1700s.

Smallhythe Road

The first white house on the right side of the road has a ground-floor bow window, which might signify that it once accommodated a shop. This suggests that this quiet end of the High Street might once have been the scene of more commercial activity; it was definitely the place of one of the town's major industrial enterprises, as the town tannery (*see inset*) was situated just at the far edge of the shot.

Black Horse, West Cross

This building at the west end of the High Street has undergone some remodelling and a name-change since the 1890s. Known as The Black Horse until the 1940s, the pub is now named for William Caxton, England's first commercial printer, who was reputedly born in either Tenterden or Hadlow. For about fifty years, until 1925, the pub was supplied by the town's own brewery, Edwards & Son, which was situated behind The Vine Inn.

Boorman's Stores, West Cross

Founded in 1819, Samuel Boorman's establishment soon became *the* place to shop, its success being such that, within the century, the company had expanded into premises in many of the surrounding villages. The photograph below shows the shop as it was when thriving in 1873. When Boorman's ceased trading a hundred years later, the empty premises were redeveloped as Caxton Close, the mixture of housing and shop premises visible today. Only the far right section of Boorman's original eighteenth-century property still stands.

Bennett's Yard

At the turn of the twentieth century, the Bennetts were a large family in Tenterden, running a carrier firm, coal merchant business and a bus service, which covered the route from Maidstone to Rye, taking in all the surrounding villages. By the 1920s, they were working diesel lorries as well as steam vehicles and, at one time, stabled forty horses. The yard pictured is now a quiet, private residential road, tucked well away from the main traffic of the High Street. Known as Bennetts Mews, it reveals little of the scale of its former inhabitants' enterprise.

Methodist Church

At the time of Archbishop Seeker's 1758 visitation, there were no reports of practising Methodists in Tenterden. However, it is known that there were Nonconformists meeting for worship at a farmhouse in nearby Rolvenden Layne and a Methodist church had been established in the town by 1797. This chapel, erected in 1855, was built with an additional schoolroom to allow for Sunday school teaching and this educational tradition is continued today by the preschool group that meets here.

Pittlesden, High Street

It is believed that this house, reputed to be the oldest in Tenterden, was one of three gatehouses belonging to the fourteenth-century Pittlesden manor house (now demolished). Rescued from the threat of demolition itself in the 1950s, the house has been well preserved and retains a wealth of original features. To the rear is a later extension, thought to have been added in the 1500s, but the original divisions of hall and service, with a skylight above, can still be seen in the main body of the building.

Town Pump, High Street

The town pump would have been used by farmers and stockmen to water their horses and livestock at the Tenterden markets. It would also have been used by residents without access to other sources of potable water. At the time this photograph was taken, in the early 1900s, domestic tap water was an expensive luxury; it was not until the 1930s, with the mass manufacture of copper piping, that a fixed domestic water supply became a realistic option for the majority of homes in Britain.

Tenterden Library

Over the years, there have been public libraries located at various buildings in the town and many of these have been run by local individuals as private enterprises. During the interwar period, the County Education Committee provided a mobile library, which served the rural districts. Today's modern library space is shared with the town's post office and information centre at the Tenterden Gateway.

E. J. Mercer, Station Road

The Mercer family kept a number of shops in Tenterden throughout the nineteenth and twentieth centuries. Mr E. Mercer is recorded as a seed merchant and a barber, and he also ran a greengrocer's in the High Street. Ellen Mercer (pictured below) was the wife of John, who ran a coal carter's business. Their son, Reuben, was killed in action with the RAF in 1941, and is buried in the town cemetery.

High Street View, West to East

Apart from the obvious changes to the shopfronts, fashion and transport, perhaps the most notable difference between these two shots of the same stretch of the High Street is the absence of chimneys from today's roofline. Clearly evidence of a move away from solid fuel energy sources, this also shows how the occupation of High Street premises has changed in the last century, as very few of the shops today still provide domestic accommodation for owners and staff.

Borough Place

This was Tenterden's workhouse, built on the site of the Elizabethan poorhouse. In the 1830s, the Poor Law Commissioners agreed to enlarge the existing poorhouse, and a new workhouse – for some time, the West View Hospital – was built in 1843. In the 1700s, the workhouse apothecary, Jeremiah Cliff, kept records of the deaths of the town's inhabitants – including a member of his own household staff, who hanged herself at his home, Cliff House, next door to the Town Hall, in 1722.

Tenterden Fire Station, High Street

It was the position of the fire station that was the key to its demise in 1972. The 1823 Market Hall served early firefighters well, and the horses that used to pull the engines were comfortably stabled in a yard behind. However, the scale of modern equipment, as well as increases in town traffic, made this an impractical base for the twentieth century and the new station was located in a more easily accessible spot outside the main town, next to Homewood School.

Cattle on High Street Greens, *c.* 1900
This photograph shows the extent of the High Street greens at the turn of the twentieth century and provides evidence for the road's former name of 'Broad Tenterden'. Today, the small areas of the remaining greens provide some ornament to the busy High Street, which has been adapted to suit traffic of a four-wheeled, rather than four-hoofed, variety.

High Street Greens Stock Market, *c.* 1890s

Throughout the nineteenth century, a weekly stock market was held here and an annual stock fair, first recorded in the 1200s, was held on the first Monday of May until 1977. The Tenterden May Fair survived far longer than many of its local counterparts, relocating to the recreation ground between the wars. Although now much diminished, these green areas are, in fact, remnants of Saxon common land and are a distinctive feature of this area of Kent.

Bishop's Yard
The two houses that stand adjacent to the Zion Baptist chapel were built, in 1874, on the site of this timber-framed Tudor building. At the time of the earlier photograph, the building was the business premises of stonemasons, Stephen Bishop and Henry Pennells.

Zion Baptist Church, High Street

There is a strong tradition of Nonconformist worship in Tenterden and evidence that a number of Baptist meeting houses were licensed in the town in the 1600s. This church, originally built in 1835, succeeded a Protestant Dissenters' meeting house in Bell's Lane (then Honey Lane), which had been established in 1767. Remodelled in 1887, the church has changed very little in the intervening century.

Outside The Vine Inn

The photograph below shows a town on the brink of modernisation. The telegraph poles were introduced in the years leading up to the First World War and, although there are no cars in the shot, the premises of Pratt's Motors can be seen on the left-hand side. The Vine Inn is an eighteenth-century building with a Victorian façade. In the area behind the pub, the Edwards family ran a brewery, which supplied all the pubs in the town until it was dismantled in 1925.

Site of Town Market House

This interesting photograph shows rebuilding work in the 1960s. This open space was once the site of the town's medieval market house, until its demolition in the 1820s. This would have been the hub of town life, especially during the Commonwealth, when the state took over the role of the Church in publishing marriage notices. This was also the site of Tenterden town stocks.

The White Lion

It is probable that this building was the 'Whyte Lyon' inn referred to in a 1623 account of the town. Its current façade – white-painted mathematical tiling – belies the building's actual age, which its interior oak-beamed structure suggests might be over 400 years. It has seen a number of changes of use over its long lifetime and is pictured here during the late nineteenth century, when it served as the town's post office.

Nos 64–66 High Street

Originally dating from the eighteenth century, this building was redesigned in the 1840s and its appearance has changed little since. It has been the premises of many different shops and local businesses and was, for some forty years, the town's post office.

Nos 60–62 High Street

This is one of the oldest buildings in the town, with a history that can be traced as far back as the 1480s. It has accommodated a variety of businesses, including a number of pharmacies – the trade identified by Mr Ridley's bull's-eye lantern hanging outside. Ridley was a chemist and photographer who published a celebrated series of picture postcards of Tenterden, while one of his regular portrait clients was Dame Ellen Terry, who lived at nearby Smallhythe Place.

County Bank

This grand building of 1866 was a purpose-built branch of the London and County Bank (locally known as the Farmers' Bank due to the predominance of that occupation among its clients). As well as the banking facilities on the ground floor, accommodation was provided on the upper two storeys for the bank manager and his family.

Town Toll Gate and Police Station, High Street
The wooden toll house, which was built with the tollgate in 1762, also served as the town's lock-up until it was replaced, when the toll gate was removed in 1880, by the brick-built police station.

Nos 47–49 High Street, Tenterden

A cycle shop occupied the premises of No. 49 for around a decade between the start of the First World War and the late 1920s, and Winter's ladies' outfitters was a thriving business at No. 47 for over half a century. However, this building is of fifteenth- or sixteenth-century origin and, inside, its fireplaces, window bays, staircases and passageways give clear evidence of its former role as a domestic dwelling.

The Old Grammar School

A hall house from the 1400s, this building functioned as a school for 300 years, from 1521, when it was already considered 'very ancient', until the National Schools took over the responsibility for children's education. In the 1500s, it was the duty of the chantry priest of St Mildred's to 'teche his scolers accordingly' and he was supported, at least partially, by an endowment from the Woolpack Inn. Since the 1800s, the building has served as shops and accommodation.

The Drill Hall

Erected in 1911 at a cost of £1,000 for the use of the 5th Territorial Force Battalion East Kent Regiment, this building has since been adopted by the St Mildred's and now serves as one of the church halls.

St Mildred's Church, Tenterden's 'Pocket Cathedral'

One of only three churches in the county dedicated to St Mildred, this 'pocket cathedral' was instituted in 1180 and greatly enlarged and improved with the profits of the local wool trade during the fifteenth century. Its spiritual role might have altered over its lifetime, but the church has been an integral part of the life of the town, which has prospered in its shadow, for over 800 years.

St Mildred's Church Tower

This view gives some idea of the scale of the tower, from which it is possible to see the French Coast on clear days. Its unusual fifteenth-century double west doorway is one of only two in the county. Legend has it that funds used to build the tower were diverted away from coastal defences, leading to the tragedy of the Goodwin Sands. The story is a fiction but there is a positive connection with the sea, as shells gathered at Rye in 1709 were used in the tower's mortar.

View from Top of St Mildred's Church Tower, Looking East
Without its fringe of chestnut trees, the High Street in 1890 looks somewhat stark and exposed compared with the same view today. Clearly, the majority of development has been in-filling between Ivy Court and East Cross. To the far right, in the middle distance can be seen the oast houses and chimneys of Hales Place, today just barely visible among the trees.

View from Top of St Mildred's Church Tower, Looking West
The spindly chestnut saplings have matured and some of the expanse of the High Street greens has given way to tarmac, but the outward appearances of many of the High Street buildings, photographed here in 1900, have hardly altered in the intervening century and may be clearly discerned today.

View from Top of St Mildred's Church Tower, Looking South-West
This busy stretch of the High Street has become increasingly commercialised since 1900; perhaps most notable in this photograph are the private houses (bottom right corner) that have all been redeveloped as retail premises. Overall, there has not been a great deal of expansion away from the town's main roads – one notable exception to this being the supermarket and car-park development seen at the top right-hand corner of the recent picture.

View North-East from St Mildred's Church Tower, Showing KESR Station at Tenterden
Between the times of its opening in the early 1900s and closure in 1954, the Kent and East Sussex Light Railway (KESR) ran between Robertsbridge and Headcorn, stopping at a station in the centre of Tenterden. Today, a group of dedicated and skilled enthusiasts maintains 10½ miles of the line and the engines and carriages that pass along it, some of which can be seen in the middle distance of this picture, in the station sidings.

Woolpack Hotel, High Street

In the 1500s, 'the Wolsake' is known to have provided an endowment to support the chaplain at St Mildred's church, and the pub was the resting place of choice for bishops visiting the town. The inn's card room (later known as the Mayor's Parlour) was annexed in the building of the eighteenth-century town hall, a hidden door (now cleverly disguised) allowing for access between the two buildings. The high yard entrance, designed to admit coaches, is a common feature of the older Tenterden buildings.

Tenterden Town Hall

Built in the 1790s, this town hall was a replacement for the court hall, which was burned by the actions of prisoner Richard Burden in March 1661. The balcony was not added until 1912, when the beautiful Venetian window was removed. Fortunately, this was restored in the 1970s, at which time the assembly room was also refurbished.

Sheep Pens in High Street

This very early photograph dates from the 1860s. Although faded, it is possible to pick out the farmers' top hats and shepherds' smocks. This area of the High Street has been a central assembly point since the medieval period; in fact, there is record of stalls or early shops being erected in front of the church as early as 1279.

Bells Lane (Formerly Honey Lane)
Today, this beautifully appointed little lane of quiet cottages presents a picture of elegant serenity. However, a hundred years ago, Bells Lane was notorious for the drunken and violent behaviour of its inhabitants. The town's theatre stood here in the late 1700s and the three cottages on the site today are named to mark this dramatic heritage. It is also believed that the house known as Chapel Cottage was the location of Tenterden's first Baptist meeting house, established in 1767.

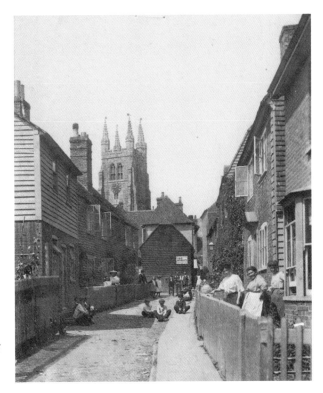

Nos 29–33, High Street

This Wealden hall house, dating from the fourteenth century, has served many purposes during its lifetime. One of its occupiers was Stephen Hook, the butcher, whose impressive array of Christmas produce for 1902 is shown here (*inset*). The building has been well preserved inside as well as out, its low, beamed ceilings, panelled walls, open fireplaces and original carved doorway giving a sense of its role as a wealthy cloth merchant's home during the Tudor period.

No. 32 High Street
At the time this photograph was taken, the building with the ornate balcony and windows was the chemist shop of Henry Meynell. With his wife and daughter, he ran his business for over fifty years, having moved into the premises in 1900. Many people in the town thought of Mr Meynell as their local doctor.

Harris Arms Inn

The high, arched passageway, which would have once admitted horse-drawn carriages to the stable yard at the centre of this long building, still exists as the entrance to a service alley between two shops. The Harris Arms ceased trading in the late 1800s but the premises have been in constant use, one end having been rebuilt as a Woolworths branch in the 1950s.

Nos 8–10 High Street

It is thought that this building marks the extent of St Mildred's glebelands. The alleyway to its left was the town rope-walk. During Tenterden's association with the Cinque Ports, the production of rope, for use in shipbuilding, would have been a strong local industry. There has been much alteration to these premises, but their origins are probably seventeenth century or earlier. It was to here that Mr Apps relocated his business when his former shop was demolished to accommodate the new County Bank in 1867.

Ivy Court

Built in 1761, this once elegant house is barely distinguishable behind its modern shop façade. The Embassy cinema was built in 1938, the front garden made way for the shop fronts visible today and the rear garden now provides the majority of the town's car-parking space. Inside, the tall sash windows and elegant fireplaces still give some sense of the house's former grandeur.

Eastwell House
These shops replaced Eastwell House, which can be seen behind the cart in the earlier picture. During the building project in the early 1960s, a painted floral pattern was found on one of the walls – a fragment of Tudor interior design.

East Cross

This unusual photograph shows a horse sale at East Cross greens and on the area that was later to become the recreation ground. Owners, buyers, sellers and handlers jostle with the animals where, today, there is orderly traffic control.

Recreation Ground

When the annual fair became too large and noisy for the High Street greens, alternative accommodation was found in the glebe fields, from which the large recreation ground was created.

East Cross and Armoury

Many of the large eighteenth- and nineteenth-century houses in this area are today occupied as shops and businesses. East Cross has undergone much development during the twentieth century, part of which was the joint effort of the Women's Voluntary Service and the Rotary Club to create the beautiful East Cross Garden in 1948.

Picture Theatre, Oaks Road

Tenterden's first cinema, affectionately known as the 'Picture Palace', opened in 1912. At the turn of the century, with its state-of-the-art equipment and design, this was the finest cinema in the South East. Indeed, its success was such that its owners built a larger theatre (the 800-seat Embassy) across the road in 1936. Having served as an Army depot during the war and survived the threat of demolition in the 1950s, the building today, now known as The Fairings, is now occupied by a variety of shops and businesses.

Golden Cross, Golden Square

This area, though not really a square, marks a meeting of the main roads into and out of Tenterden. The smaller house pictured, Plough Cottage, was possibly a Tudor barn, converted when the larger house was built in 1762. For many years, this smaller building was a popular pub, known as The Plough, until it closed, along with a number of other small pubs and alehouses in the town, in 1918.

Oaks Road

The eponymous trees have matured and the mode of transport has changed, but little else has altered in Oaks Road over the last century; it remains an elegant residential street on the edge of the town centre.

East Hill

This short road connects Oaks Road with the Appledore Road, forming a triangle with Golden Square. The land to left of the pictures, belonging to Hales Place, remains undeveloped and was recently planted with many deciduous trees.

Little Dane Court, Ashford Road

A house with a history, this Tudor building, for many years the premises of Mr Avery's plumbing and decorating business, is said to have been a smugglers' safe-house. There is a secret signalling window in the roof and its large fireplace hides a priest's hole, attesting to its occupants' experiences of religious turmoil in the town. It is now known affectionately by locals as 'the cat and bird house' because of the stone creatures that chase across its roof.

Westcliff, Ashford Road
In the early twentieth century, this substantial building was the Westcliff Boarding House. It later accommodated the Westcliff School, but this closed in 1957 and the premises were bought by the current occupiers in the 1970s.

Tower House, Ashford Road

This house dates from the beginning of the nineteenth century; its folly tower, from which a view of the coast is possible, was a later addition. The façade of this house is constructed in a similar way to that of The Pebbles in the High Street; it is faced with wooden panels, which are stuccoed to make them look like stonework.

The White House, Ashford Road

The Venetian windows and pedimented doorframe of this Palladian-style house remain as clean and elegant today as when they were first erected, confirming the White House's status as one of the finest examples of the architectural sophistication that abounds in Tenterden.

Unitarian Chapel

Unitarian groups emerged during the early 1700s, when there was discord over the restored monarchy's Act of Uniformity. In Tenterden, a distinct Unitarian church was established by Revd Hawe in 1662. This church was built in 1746 on a site known as the Meeting House Field, and is one of a handful of similar 'private house'-style chapels, deliberately modest and discreet, in the locality. In 1783, while visiting his preacher friend, Joseph Priestly, Benjamin Franklin sat among the church's congregation.

Penderell Court and Parsonage House

This pair of houses dates from 1769 and, like many others in the town, they are of timber-frame construction, faced with the distinctive mathematical tiles. These tiles are designed to look like bricks when hanging, but were considerably cheaper during the early 1800s when bricks were highly taxed. From 1918 until 1970, Penderell Court served as a school for some time under the leadership of Miss Hall.

Clifton House, Ashford Road

In November 1914, this house (built in 1873) opened its doors as a military hospital and welcomed fifteen wounded Belgian soldiers – the first of many who would be nursed by Dr Dring and his staff of Volunteer Aid Detachment nurses. The people of Tenterden rallied to support the hospital, contributing beds, furniture and motor transport as well as food and gifts for the soldiers. Ironically, this peaceful view of rural life around Clifton House was taken during the war or just before its outbreak.

Beacon Oak Road

This road links the Appledore and Ashford Roads, its elegant Victorian houses now somewhat cramped by parked cars and passing traffic. In or near this area, before the present houses were built, was once the site of the town pound.

Homewood House

This house was built by James Haffenden in the 1760s. From 1875, it was home to a dame school, until the estate was bought by the Admiral Sir Charles Drury in 1910, at which time it reverted to its function as a private home. However, in 1947, Lady Drury sold the house and grounds to the KCC Education Committee, with the express instruction that its role as an educational establishment should be restored, and Homewood School welcomed its first pupils in 1949.

Silver Hill

This area was severely damaged by bombing during the 1940s and the more modern cottages (Nos 1–7) were built during redevelopment of the site. A public footpath is hidden away behind the houses.

St Michael and All Angels' Church, Ashford Road

In the 1860s, Tenterden's curate, Revd Tress Beale, had little choice but to preach sermons at the wheelwright's in Boresisle (as the area of St Michael's was then known) until his father, Seaman Beale, commissioned the building of a National School in 1862. For some months, Sunday services took place in the village school but, the following year, Beale organised – and largely financed – a second ambitious building project; the church of St Michael and All Angels was consecrated on 1 August.

Jireh Chapel, Ashford Road, St Michael's

This building is the fourth meeting chapel of the Strict Baptist congregation, and the third named 'Jireh'; the first recorded meeting place was referred to as 'Salem' (although the location of this early chapel is unknown). The chapel opened on 20 October 1869 and is still in service today. Reuben Weeks (pictured here) was pastor of the chapel between 1884 and 1922.

Ashford Road, Looking North, St Michael's

The main road through the village is flanked by two important buildings: The Crown Inn and the toll house (now a private residence). Both date from the nineteenth century, during the area's major expansion from the hamlet of Boresisle to the village of St Michael's as it stands today.

St Peter & St Paul Church, Appledore

The church at Appledore is recorded in the Domesday Monachorum, but nothing of this early (possibly wood and thatch) structure remains. In 1380, French raiders, having attacked other coastal towns in the 1370s, set fire to the village, an act of aggression that left its scars; there are scorch marks around the church doors and, during maintenance work in the 1920s, charred embers were found beneath the church floor. Much restoration work was done during the late nineteenth and early twentieth centuries.

The Red Lion, Appledore

William Noakes, an Appledore man, took on the Red Lion (or Lion) Inn during the 1870s with his wife and young family. Forty years later, he was still the publican, now augmenting his business with horse and trap for hire. The current Black Lion pub stands on the site of the Red Lion, just in front of parish church, at the head of the main street.

Cattle in the Main Street, Appledore

This photograph dates from sometime between the 1870s and 1900, the period of William Sims' occupancy of the shop. In this rural area, the livelihood of which was traditionally founded on farming, a scene like this in the broad village High Street would not have been unusual.

Main Street, Appledore

Although it might have the look of a sleepy backwater, Appledore has stood in the front line for Kent for centuries. Fortified as recently as the Second World War, its canal (*inset*) was originally built as a means of defence against Napoleon's troops. Attacked by the French in the fourteenth century and invaded by Vikings in the ninth, the village has endured and, in the county's own great uprisings, Appledore fielded men of courage to march with both Watt Tyler and Jack Cade.

Main Street, Appledore

During the extreme poverty of the early nineteenth century, a number of Appledore residents had seized the opportunity to emigrate. However, by the late 1800s, the village was growing and people were beginning to move here to enjoy their retirement. This increasing popularity and prosperity is clear from the photograph of the wide main road, its large, bay-fronted houses and brick-paved path creating an air of provincial elegance.

APPLEDORE.

St George's Church, Benenden

Benenden is one of the Kent villages named in the Domesday Book, and there was a church on this site in the eleventh century. However, the current building is far more recent than that, as a fire in 1672 completely destroyed the existing church, its tower and bells and five adjoining houses. The new church was erected in 1677/78, with further improvements made over the eighteenth and nineteenth centuries.

The Bull Inn, Benenden

The Bull was built at the turn of the seventeenth century and altered and extended during the nineteenth. From the 1870s, the inn (sometimes referred to as The Bull Hotel) was run by Charles and Susanna Buckett with their large family. Over four centuries, the pub has witnessed the development of Benenden from a sparsely populated wealden den into the village we know today, largely created by the patronage of Lord Cranbrook in the mid-1800s.

Benenden Green

Formerly known as The Playstool, Benenden Green has been associated with the game of cricket for over a century and the village has fielded a number of its own champion cricketers, such as Richard Mills and Edward Wenman. The centre building pictured is the school founded by Edmund Gibbons in 1609, which still serves the village community today as the primary school early years unit.

St Margaret's Church, Bethersden
Although a church at Bethersden is mentioned in the Domesday Monochorum, the existing one dates from the fourteenth and fifteenth centuries. Enthusiastic nineteenth-century 'restoration' in Bath stone has obscured some of the Kentish ragstone masonry, but there is very little here of the famous Bethersden 'marble' that is used so widely in the county's cathedrals and other churches. The church's vaults provide final resting places for members of the influential Lovelace family who resided here.

High Street and The George Inn, Bethersden

At the time of the 1911 census, the George Inn was run by William and Mary Philpott, who lived here with their seven children. Beyond the pub can be seen the sign for Padgham's, Grocer and Baker. Today, the High Street is still bustling, although now with traffic as well as people.

The Post Office, Bethersden
This nineteenth-century building was, at the turn of the twentieth century, a branch of Boorman's Stores, based in Tenterden High Street.

Forge Corner, Bethersden

A few early motor vehicles on the A28 Ashford Road. The long, white agricultural building to the far left of the picture has found a new lease of life; it is now home to the Stevenson Brothers' workshop.

The Bull Inn, Bethersden

This inn has served travellers on the Ashford–Tenterden road since 1645 and, though the building has undergone extensive refurbishment in more recent years, it retains many original features, such as its inglenook fireplace. On the opposite side of the road stands the pub's stables and coach-house. This small, square building has provided accommodation for the village's criminals – a court and coroner's court being held, at one time, in the pub – and was also used by the local Home Guard as a training centre during the Second World War.

All Saints' Church, Biddenden

The main part of the church, which has been altered and enlarged throughout its lifetime, was built during the 1200s and 1300s, but there is evidence to suggest a church stood here at the time of the Norman Conquest. The church houses a famous collection of memorial brasses and has an exterior stair turret.

View of Biddenden High Street, Towards the A274

This view shows the High Street at the turn of the twentieth century. On the far right of the early picture can be seen the frame used by the wheelwright for shaping and fixing cartwheels (some examples of which are propped against the wall). Today, the area is fenced inside the garden of the building, which is now a private house. The paving is Bethersden marble, excavated locally.

View of Biddenden High Street, Towards All Saints' Church

The horse-drawn cart almost obscures the hint of the future that appears towards the back of this earlier picture – one of the first motor cars in the area. The deep-roofed High Street buildings were constructed to accommodate the weaving industry of the 1300s and many still have interconnecting attic rooms.

Clothworkers' Hall, Biddenden

During the fifteenth century, when the broadcloth industry was at its height in this area of the Weald, this building provided both workshop and accommodation for some of Biddenden's weavers. At some point, it was divided on its ground and first floors into eight separate dwellings, but the attic (which was designed to accommodate a large loom) remained an open space, spanning the length of the building.

Church Hill, Greenside, High Halden

High Halden is one of the area's longest inhabited places. Situated on the very outskirts of the Wealden forest and the edge of the Romney Marsh, perhaps it was this location that made it a popular smugglers' haunt. It is believed that the notorious Hawkhurst Gang frequented The Chequers Inn during the 1700s, but the building (currently undergoing refurbishment) has a history that can be traced back to the 1620s.

Millfield, High Halden

Like so many in the area, the village mill at High Halden, which was a post mill, used for cereal grinding, was lost to the attentions of George 'Mill Smasher' Jarvis, who also dismantled the mills at nearby Appledore and Headcorn. The mill survived until the turn of the twentieth century, but its site has now been transformed into a residential road.

The Church of St Mary the Virgin, Rolvenden

Although this church dates from the early 1200s, there is record of a Saxon church here from as early as 1090. This was the living of Revd John Frankesh at the time of his martyrdom in Canterbury, in 1555. It features an unusual 'squire's pew', which is actually a small room, situated in a gallery overlooking the south chapel, and was furnished for the comfort and private devotions of the Gibbons family from nearby Hole Park.

Wesley's House, Rolvenden Layne

This is the building, then known as Layne Farmhouse, from which John Wesley preached his Methodist doctrine in the 1750s and 1760s, and it was here that Wesley and his followers were arrested by Justice Monypenny in 1760. After an appeal to the King's Court, these convictions were quashed, and Wesley often referred to his experiences at Rolvenden as a key turning point in the development of Methodism in Britain.

The Windmill, Rolvenden

There is reference to a mill here from as early as the 1550s and its history as a working mill can be traced from that time until the 1880s, when the sails were removed. During the 1900s, the mill fell into dereliction but was saved in the 1950s by the Barham family and, since its restoration, the mill has found fame appearing in film and television programmes.

Smallhythe Place

The house, which was home to Dame Ellen Terry from 1899, was possibly built after a fire burned much of Smallhythe in 1514. The house is unusual in its construction and it is believed that it might have been constructed as a public building; possibly a court house, inn or the office of shipbuilder, it might even have served as accommodation for the local priest. On the first floor, there is an interesting window frame made from the recycled timbers of a galleon.

Smallhythe Ferry Crossing

The Rother separated Smallhythe and the Isle of Oxney from the rest of the Weald and before the redirection of the river, ferries were the only means by which people could enter or exit the island. William Cobbett described the island as being wreathed in thick fog, so it is hardly surprising that this secret, hidden place was once a popular smugglers' haunt. Today, the river here is a much diminished waterway known as the Reading Sewer, and its ferries have been replaced by bridges.

Priest's House, Smallhythe

During the early 1500s, Smallhythe suffered a terrible fire that destroyed its church; this house was erected at the time the church was rebuilt. It was to become the home and workplace of Robert Brigandyne, Henry VIII's clerk of ships, and the man appointed to supervise the construction of the *Mary Rose* in 1510.

The Street, Wittersham

In 1911, this building, known as the Church Bakery, was both a bakery and a post office, run by Frank Stanford, who lived here with his family and staff. Charles Payne, whose cart is pictured, was a local carrier living in Back Street with his wife and four children. A hundred years ago, this would have been a hub of village life; today, it is a private residence in a peaceful village street.

Poplar Road, Wittersham

This image probably shows a member of the Sweatman family, who were the proprietors of Wittersham Forge at the turn of the twentieth century. The wheels propped against the building are evidence of the forge's trade, and the emblem on the wall above is the emblem of the BSA cycle and motorcycle company. Today's car repair workshop continues the forge's tradition of vehicle maintenance.

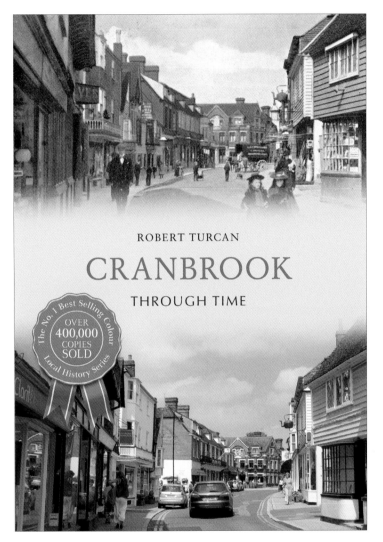

Cranbrook Through Time

Robert Turcan

This fascinating selection of photographs traces some of the many ways in which Cranbrook has changed and developed over the last century.

978 1 4456 0823 5
96 pages, full colour

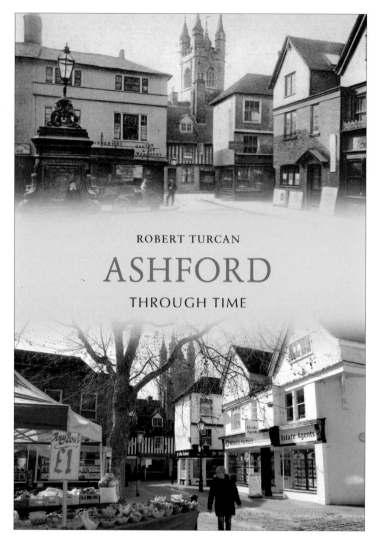